UKULELE
Sing & Strum Fun Book

written and illustrated by

Jerrold Connors

an Alligator Boogaloo production

Jiminy Kokopo's Ukulele Sing and Strum Fun Book

was written and illustrated by

Jerrold Connors

and is published by

Alligator Boogaloo
PO Box 20070
Oakland, CA 94611

The words, illustrations, and music
(unless otherwise noted) are all
© **2002**
by Jerrold Connors

This book is catalogued under the
United States Library of Congress Control Number:

2002092170

and under the International Standard Book Number:

0-9721416-0-X

This book was

printed in the United States

on

recycled paper

and is lovingly dedicated to

Kristen Batten

TABLE OF CONTENTS

Introduction 4
About the Ukulele 5
Choosing a Ukulele 6
Taking Care of your Uke 6
Ukulele Diagram 7
Holding the Uke 8
Strumming the Uke 9
Tuning Your Uke 10
Using this Book 11
Music Basics 12
The Music Scale 13
Basic Melody Playing 14
   Little Brown Jug 14
   Funky Little Uke Tune 15
Harmony Playing 16
   Aloha `Oe 16
Chord Playing 17
Chord Family: C Major 18
   Little Brown Jug 19
   She'll Be Comin' 20
   Old Folks at Home 21
Chord Family: F Major 22
   The Alphabet Song 23
   Pet Shop Hoedown 24
Rhythm and Strumming 26
Chord Family: D Major 27
   My Love for You Is a Gaga Gugu 28
Transposing 30
Chord Family: G Major 31
   The Mongoose Shuffle 32
Chord Family: A Major 34
   Your Momma Wears Army Boots 35
   Old Lunchroom Blues 36
Ukulele Puzzles 37
Introductions, Endings & Flourishes 38
Chord Family: B Major 40
Chord Family: E Major 41
   My Grandfather's Clock 42
Be a Ukulele Hero 43
Tips on Showmanship 44
Improvising Melodies 44
   Jackson is a Monkey 45
Jiminy's Big List of Uke Chords 46
Ukulele Puzzle Answers 48

INTRODUCTION

Hi, my name is Jiminy Kokopo and I am here to teach you how to play the uke.

Now some people might say when they see you pick up a ukulele, "Hey! Look at Tiny Tim over there!" or "Wassa matter? Your guitar shrink in the wash or sumpin'?" And maybe they will think that you can only play "My Dog Has Fleas" and "Camptown Races." And if you're the extremely unlucky sort, you might even run into some jerk who takes your ukulele and pretends to paddle a boat or eat soup with it.

Well, we're going to make it so those people are sorry they ever made fun of the ukulele. Before we're through, those uke pooh-poohers will want to pick one up themselves and strum along with you.

This book will teach you the basics of uke playing, educate you about the history of this instrument, and knock some good musical sense into you. By the time you reach page 48 of this book you'll be prepared to tackle any audience and your uke playing will be the joy of all who are lucky enough to be in earshot.

So what are we waiting for? Let's throw on our best singing voices – or failing that, our loudest voices – and tune up our ukes. Here we go,

ABOUT THE UKULELE
(from *Your World Encyclopedia**)

The earliest beginnings of the instrument that would come to be known as the ukulele can be attributed to Joao Fernandes, who arrived in Honolulu on August 23, 1879 aboard the *Ravenscrag*. Thankful for a safe journey, Fernandes leaped off the ship and began playing his braguinha, a small guitar-like instrument. The braguinha was an immediate hit with the Hawaiians who heard its sharp tones.

The Portugese braguinha was adapted into something more like the ukulele we know by Manuel Nunez, another passenger on the *Ravenscrag*. The body was made larger and the steel strings were replaced with catgut then tuned differently. The native Hawaiian wood used to make these new instruments gave a unique sound to their playing. The wood of the koa tree was light and gave a strong resonance to the small instrument.

This new instrument was given the name "ukulele" (Hawaiian for "jumping flea") either after the way a performer's fingers jumped quickly around the fingerboard or after the skinny English performer Edward Purvis, who himself earned the nickname "Jumping Flea" due to his habit of jumping around the stage while playing his still unnamed braguinha-like instrument.

The ukulele's first formal introduction to North America came in 1915 when Hawaii opened its pavillion at the Panama-Pacific International Exposition. The ukulele had the same effect on the spectators at the Exposition as the braguinha had on the passersby at that Honolulu harbor some 150 years before. The ukulele charmed audiences and won a place in the popular music of the day.

The ukulele enjoyed a resurgence in popularity in the 1950s when the South Pacific craze swept North America. When television personality Arthur Godfrey played and endorsed ukuleles on his program, sales of the little Hawaiian instrument went through the roof.

Though often regarded as a novelty instrument, the ukulele remains one of the most popular instruments in the world. Modern performers have included the ukulele in rock and roll, jazz, and classical pieces.

Your World Encyclopedia ©1999 by Jerrold Connors

CHOOSING A UKULELE

As with any instrument, the best ukulele that you can afford should be purchased. A well made ukulele will be more reliable, easier to tune, and provide a better tone. And just like you, a good ukulele will improve with age and practice.

You will have a number of choices when you go uke shopping. The first is what size ukulele to buy. Ukuleles come in the following sizes: 21" Soprano, 23" Concert, 26" Tenor, and 30" Baritone Ukulele (this book is written for the first three types). One type of uke isn't necessarily better than another, but you will probably find the soprano uke easiest to come by.

You will also have to choose what shape ukulele you want. You will usually have a choice between the traditional (guitar) shape and the "pineapple" shape. The difference here is that the pineapple uke is a little louder. Ukuleles may also come in novelty shapes like peanuts, watermelons, giant clams, and cans of soup. While these are fun to look at, they are sometimes awkward to play and usually quite expensive. Much less expensive are ukuleles emblazoned with palm trees, sunsets, and the words "Aloha from Hawaii." These are made for tourists and better suited to hanging on a wall than playing.

The material of the uke should also be taken into consideration. The most expensive ukes are made of the very resonant Hawaiian koa wood. Many beginner ukes are made of mahogany, which gives a similarly rich sound. If you are going to spend as much time with your uke as I hope you will, buy a uke that feels good to you. Don't forget, some of the best musicians started playing on ukuleles made of cigar boxes and rubber bands – a 26" Koa wood tenor ukulele shaped like Tiny Tim's head isn't going to make you a better player. Only practice and having fun will do that.

Finally, some good places to find ukuleles are at garage sales, pawn shops, and online auctions. When buying a used ukulele pay attention to the following things:

- the uke should be free of cracks or gouges in the wood (a few light scratches won't hurt)
- the sides of the uke's body should be glued firmly to the front and back
- the bridge should be fixed into position and not swivel, shimmy, or shake
- the tuning pegs should not slip (they can be replaced)
- and like your own, the uke's neck should be connected firmly to its body

TAKING CARE OF YOUR UKE

Here are the top tips to keep your uke in tip-top condition, fail to follow these tips and your uke will fall to pot and that's the pits:

- wash your hands before picking up your uke
- keep your uke away from water and humidity
- store your uke in its protective case
- use a soft cloth to wipe your uke clean regularly
- never use a peanut butter sandwich as a pick

UKULELE DIAGRAM

All this talk about ukuleles, and we haven't even been introduced to one. The drawings below name all the parts of a ukulele for you. We will refer to these various parts as we learn how to play, so this would be a good time to get your terminology straight.

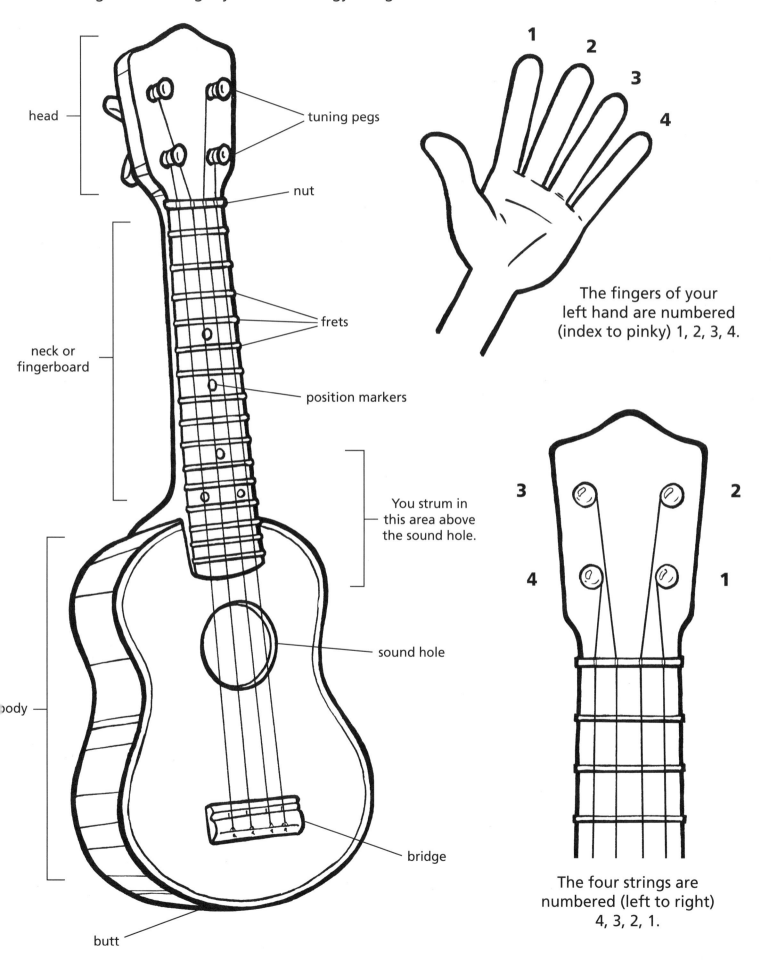

The fingers of your left hand are numbered (index to pinky) 1, 2, 3, 4.

The four strings are numbered (left to right) 4, 3, 2, 1.

HOLDING THE UKE

The ukulele is a light instrument and can be held easily while standing, jogging, or skipping rope. But don't practice that way! You should **practice while seated** so your full attention may be given to fingering and strumming as well as reading. Grab that uke and sit yourself down:

Don't play the uke angry, be relaxed. Hold that uke nice and easy.

The neck should rest in your left hand between the thumb and index finger.

Hold the uke flat against your belly with a little pressure from your right forearm.

Your fingers should come around the fingerboard such that they can reach all strings comfortably.

The lower edge of the uke may rest on your lap. (This makes playing seated easier than playing standing).

To hold and play the uke while **standing**, you should follow the same suggestions listed above. You will have to hold the uke a little more firmly against your body with your forearm to keep it from slipping.

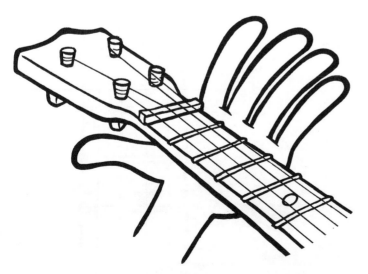

The neck of the uke should be held in the left hand. All of your fingers should be able to come up and around the neck and reach all four strings easily.

STRUMMING & PICKING THE UKE

Of the many ways to make music on your uke, **strumming** and **picking** are the two most effective. Of course, you could fill the uke with beans and shake it like a maracca but who wants to fool with beans? Better to stick with strumming and picking. Here's how you do it:

In **strumming**, all four strings are played. A repeated pattern of strumming is called a **stroke**. Below is an illustration of the Common Stroke, it consists of one strum down followed by one strum up. Both strums count as one beat. Study the pictures below and then try it on your uke.

Try to keep your right forearm as still as possible.

Make sure your fingernail faces the strings "head on."

Use the fleshy tip of your finger on the up stroke.

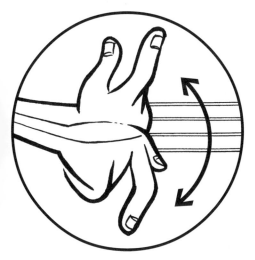

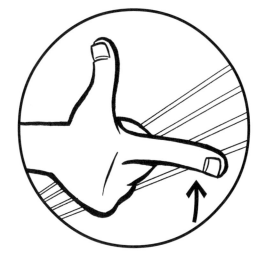

Bend your wrist inward slightly so that the tip of your index finger touches the strings.

Strike each string firmly with the front of your fingernail on the down stroke.

Limit your movement to your hand, swinging back and forth at the wrist.

A smooth strum across all four strings will give you a nice even tone. Once you are comfortable with this motion you can practice the different rhythms on page 26, or invent your own.

In **picking**, only one string is played at a time. Therefore, accuracy is of importance. Try your best to keep from hitting any string but the one indicated by the melody.

You can pick with either your thumb, index finger, or a combination of the two. And you can pick the string with either a downward or upward motion.

As in strumming, try to keep your forearm as still as possible.

For the cleanest sound, make sure your fingertip faces the strings "head on."

TUNING YOUR UKE

The songs and exercises in this book use **G-C-E-A tuning**. That means the fourth string is tuned to G, the 3rd to C, the 2nd to E, and the first to A. Knowing exactly when your uke is out of tune takes some practice. The more you play, however, the more obvious it will be when even one of your strings is out of tune. Here is the easiest method for tuning your uke.

We start with the first string, so the first thing to do is figure out exactly what "A" is. If you own a **piano**, you can use this key:

Or you can use a **Pitch Pipe** or **Ukulele Tuner**. Once you find A, tighten or loosen your first string's tuning peg until the string makes the same tone. Pluck the string firmly to make sure you are getting a clean sound. When you get that first string just right follow these steps:

This is called "tuning by ear."

Make sure the 1st string is tuned to **A**.

Then tune the 2nd string to **E**. You test this by pressing down on the 2nd string at the fifth fret. When the sound produced is the same as the open 1st string, you're in tune.

Tune the 3rd string to **C**. Test this by pressing down on the 3rd string at the fourth fret. You're in tune when it sounds the same as the open 2nd string.

Finally, tune the 4th string to **G**. Pressing down on the 4th string at the second fret should make it sound like the open 1st string.

You can double check the tuning of each of your strings using either the piano or pitch pipe. But it is best to tune the G, C, and E strings using the A string. This is the surest way to keep your uke's strings in tune with one another.

A QUICK NOTE ABOUT OLD-TIME TUNING

You may notice, if you get your hands on some old ukulele sheet music or instruction books, that the ukulele will be tuned **A - D - F# - B**. Years ago, the uke was tuned that way, but over time the G - C - E - A tuning described on this page became more popular.

You can still use those books and finger the chords as they describe, but you will have to **transpose** (or move) the names of the notes and chords down one step. So what they call **A** in those books is **G** on your uke. **B** is **A**, **C** is **B**, **D** is **C**, **E** is **D**, **F** is **E**, and **G** is **F**.

Having trouble hearing the difference between notes? **Hum** the notes as you play them. Slight differences may be more obvious in your voice than in the strings.

If you find that your uke is falling out of tune quickly and that you spend more time tuning than playing, you can **tighten the screws** at the end of the tuning pegs. This will keep them from slipping, but it will also make them harder to turn.

USING THIS BOOK

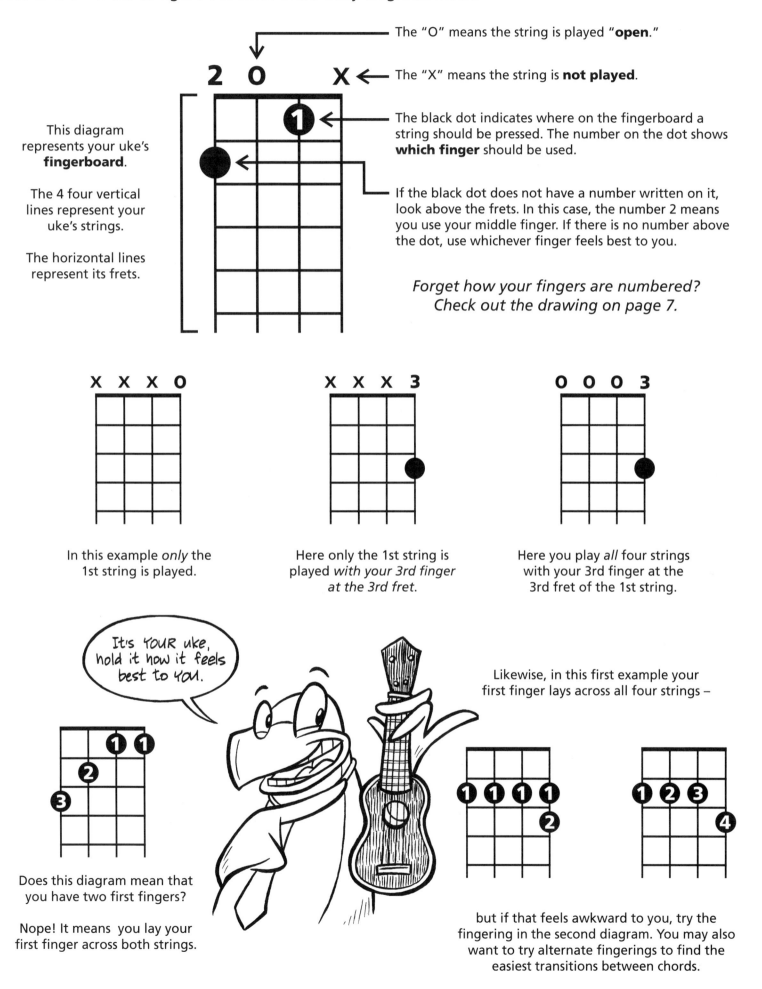

MUSIC BASICS

It isn't always necessary to understand the principles of music to enjoy playing the uke, but it helps in learning new songs and keeping your singing in tune. You should familiarize yourself with the following terms and diagrams before continuing.

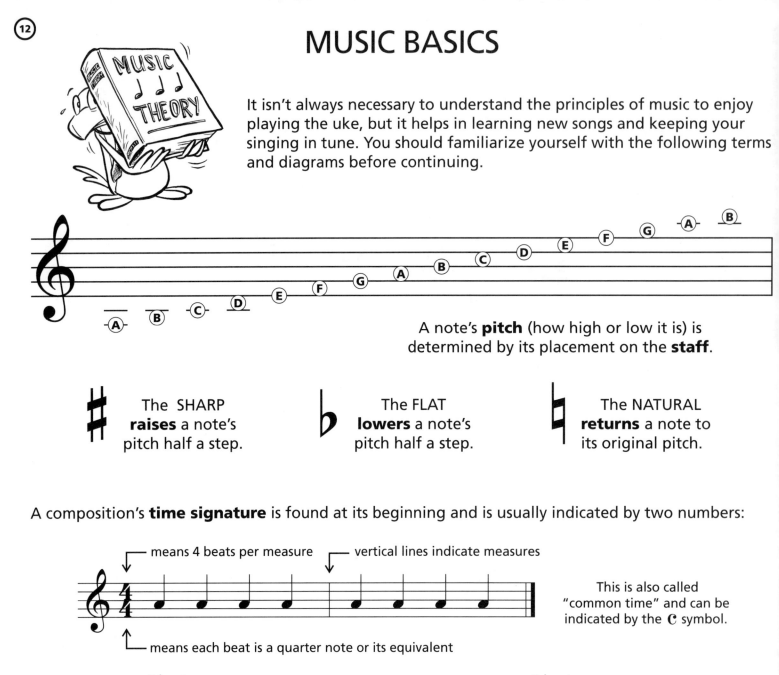

A note's **pitch** (how high or low it is) is determined by its placement on the **staff**.

The SHARP **raises** a note's pitch half a step.

The FLAT **lowers** a note's pitch half a step.

The NATURAL **returns** a note to its original pitch.

A composition's **time signature** is found at its beginning and is usually indicated by two numbers:

— means 4 beats per measure
— vertical lines indicate measures
— means each beat is a quarter note or its equivalent

This is also called "common time" and can be indicated by the 𝄴 symbol.

— means 2 beats per measure
— each beat is a quarter note or its equivalent

— means 3 beats per measure
— each beat is an eighth note or its equivalent

The relative values of different notes and rests are shown in this diagram:

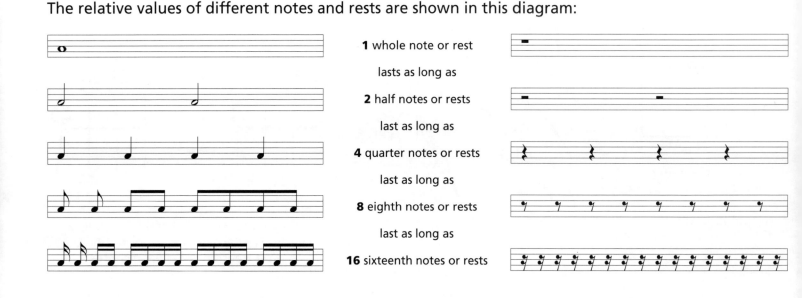

1 whole note or rest

lasts as long as

2 half notes or rests

last as long as

4 quarter notes or rests

last as long as

8 eighth notes or rests

last as long as

16 sixteenth notes or rests

THE MUSIC SCALE

We'll start with an easy exercise to help you get used to holding the uke and moving your fingers around the fingerboard. This is the **music scale**, a series of notes ascending or descending by steps and half steps. A scale can begin on any note, and will end on a note one octave higher (if ascending) or one octave lower (if descending) than the first note.

The lowest note we can reach on our uke is C (if you are tuned as described on page 10), so let's start with the C major scale. In a **major scale** the half steps occur between the 3rd and 4th and the 7th and 8th notes.

Starting on the open third string, pick every note in this diagram:

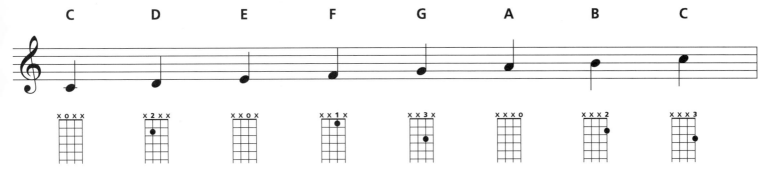

Picking up where we left off, we can squeeze another octave out of the ukulele:

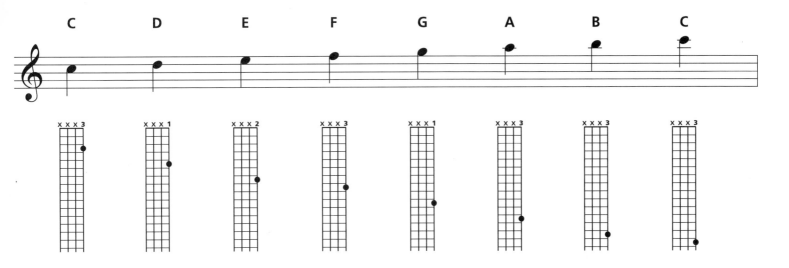

A **chromatic scale** is composed entirely of half steps. This is the C chromatic scale:

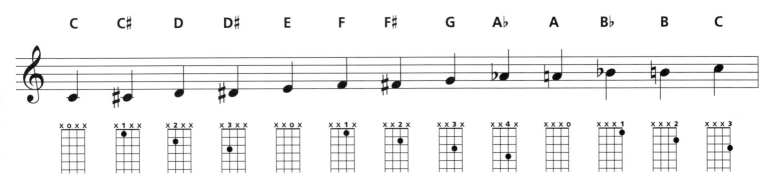

The melodies on the following three pages use this type of diagram (called tablature) to help you read and play the music. You can refer to this page at any time if you have trouble figuring out a tune.

BASIC MELODY PLAYING

We are ready to tackle our first song! Here's a popular tune, you probably know it from Saturday morning cartoons, it's:

Little Brown Jug

Traditional

Here is a little song to help you practice using the 4th string (G) instead of the 2nd string held at the 3rd fret (which is also G). Use your thumb to pluck the 4th string and your index finger to pluck the others:

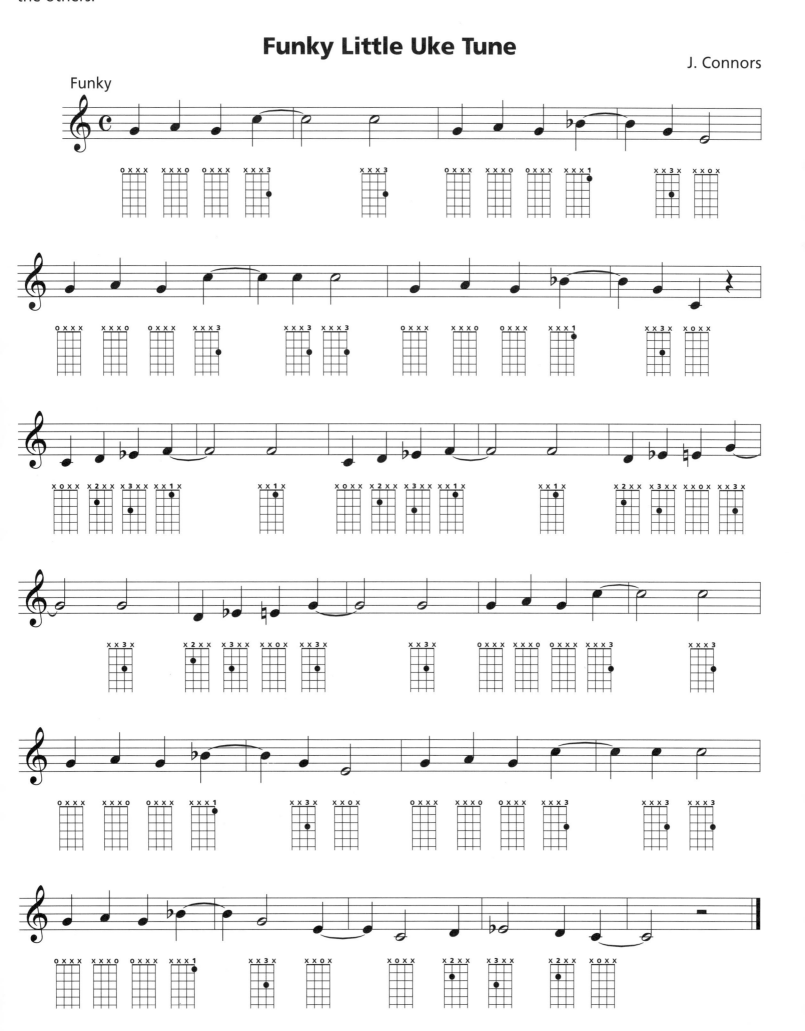

HARMONY PLAYING

Some songs are made a little more elaborate by adding extra notes played simultaneously in the melody line. This is called **harmonizing**.

In the example below, the first two notes are played as single notes, the third note, an F, gets a D played alongside it. Because they are compatible (sound nice together), the sound of the two notes being played together is called a **harmony**.

Try the harmonies in this traditional Hawaiian tune:

Aloha `Oe

H. M. Queen Lili`uokalani

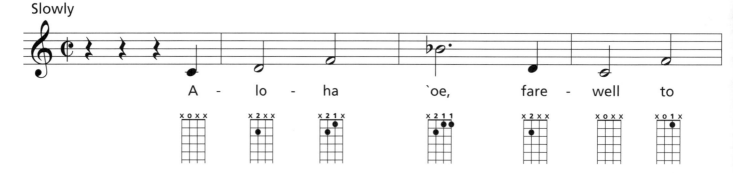

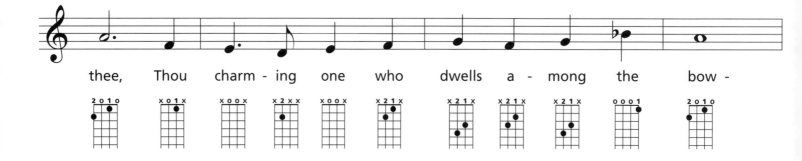

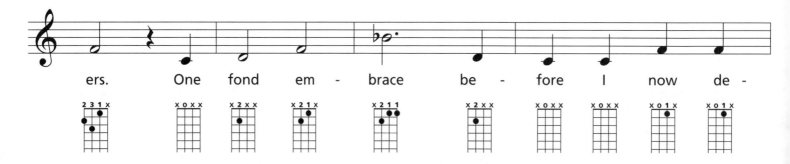

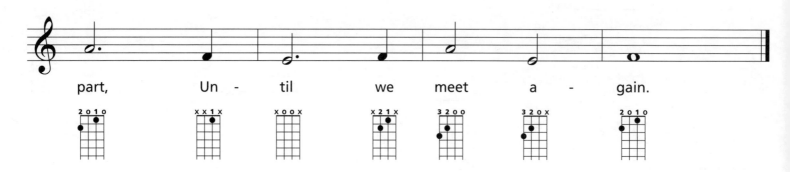

CHORD PLAYING

A **chord** is a group of three or more notes played together. You play chords on your ukulele by strumming across all four strings. Broken down, a basic chord (in this example, C major) would look like this:

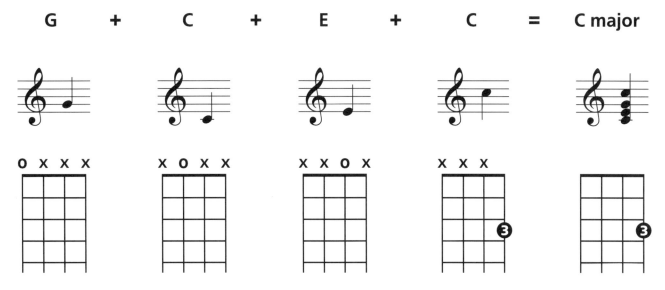

Because it is assumed all four strings are strummed, the x's and o's are not placed above chord diagrams.

You use chords to strum a song's rhythm while you sing the melody. Take the four chords below, for example. Strum each once slowly, and as you strum each chord sing the word above the diagram. Don't worry about what note you are singing, just say the word in whatever way feels natural.

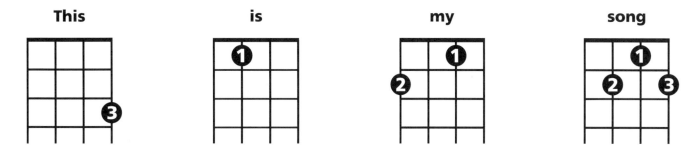

Make up a few more lines: *This is my song, It can't go wrong, Hey, there's King Kong...*

There, you just strummed your very first song. Chord playing can really be that simple. Of course, some chords will be harder to finger than others and some changes will feel awkward, but if you practice the exercises on the following pages diligently, you should be able to master them quickly enough.

As you become more comfortable with chord fingering and changes, you can try different strumming patterns (see page 26 for a few examples). Eventually, and with practice, your strumming will be the strong support of your songs and your changes will be a flawless feature of finger and fret finesse.

But for now... the exercises!

CHORD FAMILY: C MAJOR

Practice playing these chords as indicated on the music below. Strum once for each chord diagram or stroke mark (/). Concentrate more on smooth changes than on speed.

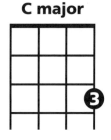
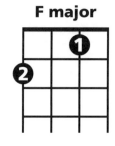
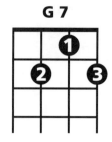

CHORD CHANGING EXERCISE

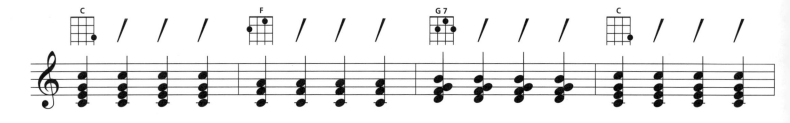
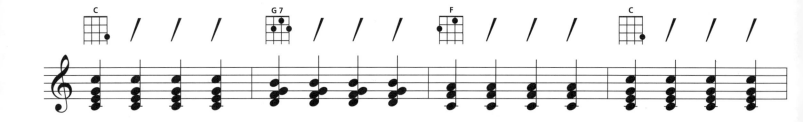
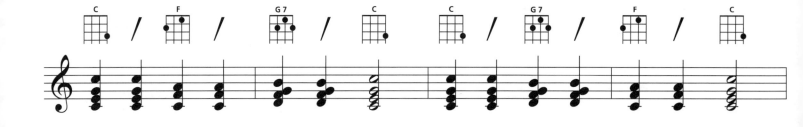
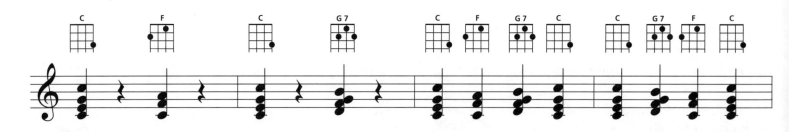

Now it is time to try out these chords on a song. Here is *Little Brown Jug* again, if you have forgotten the melody, go back to page 14 and following the fingering diagrams.

Little Brown Jug

Traditional

REMEMBER: if there are any melodies you are having trouble reading, pluck the notes out slowly on your uke using the diagrams on page 13.

She'll Be Comin'

Traditional

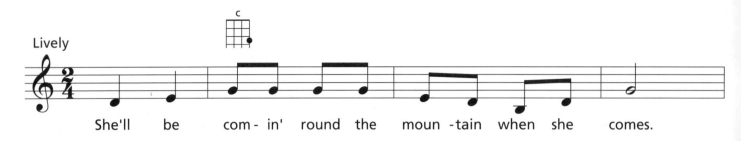

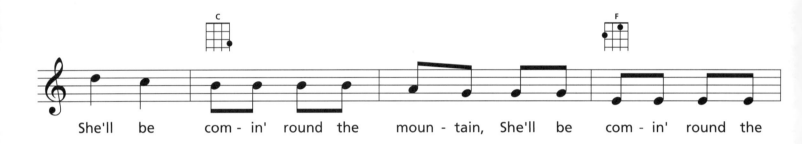
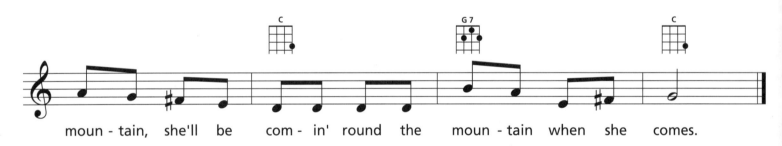

She'll be driving six white horses when she comes,
She'll be driving six white horses when she comes,
She'll be driving six white horses,
    she'll be driving six white horses,
She'll be driving six white horses when she comes.

And we'll all go down to meet her when she comes,
Yes, we'll all go down to meet her when she comes,
Oh, we'll all go down to meet her,
    I said, all go down to meet her,
Yes, we'll all go down to meet her when she comes.

And we'll all have chick'n and dumplings when she comes,
Yes we'll all have chick'n and dumplings when she comes,
Oh, we'll all have chick'n and dumplings,
    I said, all have chick'n and dumplings
Yes, we'll all have chick'n and dumplings when she comes.

CORRECTION: The music to *She'll Be Comin'* should be in the key of C.

She'll Be Comin'

Traditional

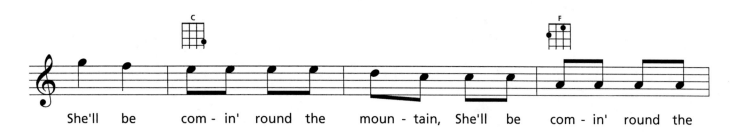
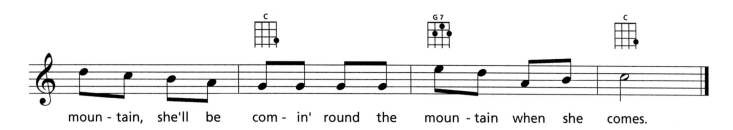

She'll be driving six white horses when she comes,
She'll be driving six white horses when she comes,
She'll be driving six white horses,
    she'll be driving six white horses,
She'll be driving six white horses when she comes.

And we'll all go down to meet her when she comes,
Yes, we'll all go down to meet her when she comes,
Oh, we'll all go down to meet her,
    I said, all go down to meet her,
Yes, we'll all go down to meet her when she comes.

And we'll all have chick'n and dumplings when she comes,
Yes we'll all have chick'n and dumplings when she comes,
Oh, we'll all have chick'n and dumplings,
    I said, all have chick'n and dumplings
Yes, we'll all have chick'n and dumplings when she comes.

©2005 by Jerrold Connors, Alligator Boogaloo, PO Box 20070, Oakland, CA 94620

CHORD FAMILY: F MAJOR

Practice playing these chords as indicated on the music below. Strum once for each chord diagram or stroke mark (/). Concentrate more on smooth changes than on speed.

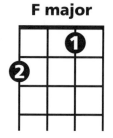
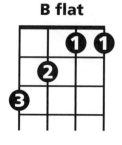
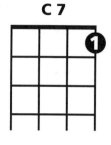

CHORD CHANGING EXERCISE

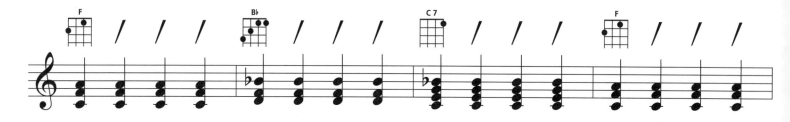

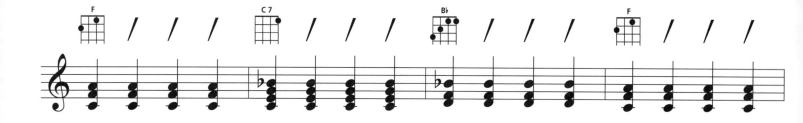

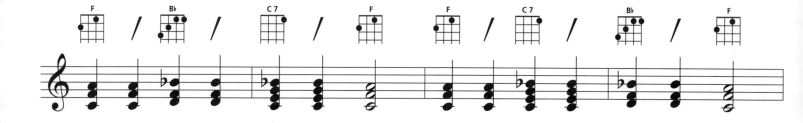

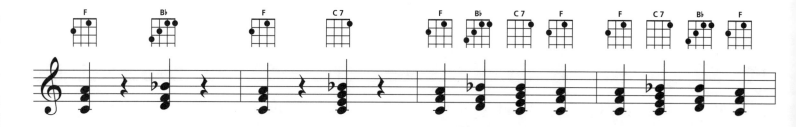

The Alphabet Song

Traditional

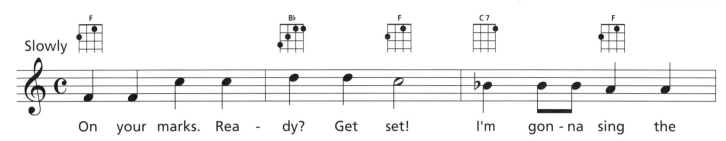

On your marks. Ready? Get set! I'm gon-na sing the

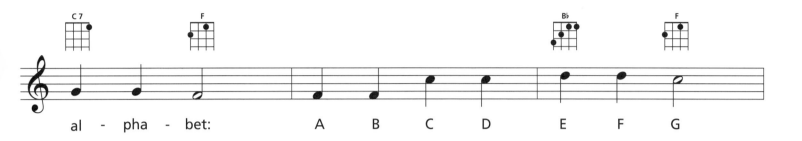

al - pha - bet: A B C D E F G

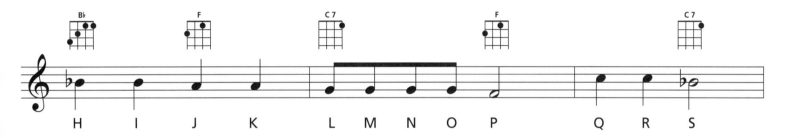

H I J K L M N O P Q R S

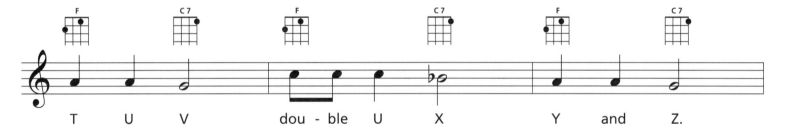

T U V dou - ble U X Y and Z.

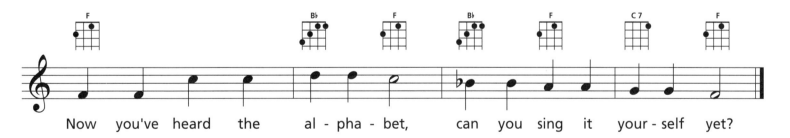

Now you've heard the al - pha - bet, can you sing it your - self yet?

MYSTERY TUNE PUZZLE! Can you figure out what tune this is? *(answer on page 48)*

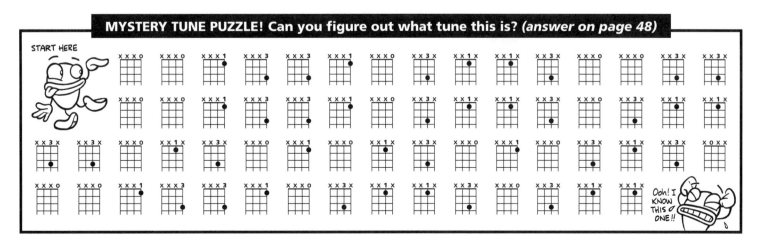

This tune is based on the old song *Whoa, Mule! Whoa!* The lyrics in the chorus of this song can go a little quickly, so be sure to take it easy until you've got them. **Then** speed it up.

Pet Shop Hoedown

traditional, arranged with new words by J. Connors

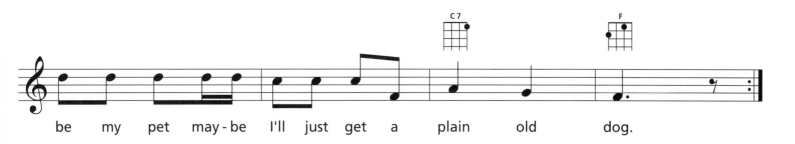

An okapi might be sloppy
And eat my mom's rose bush,
A fiddler crab isn't very drab
But it may pinch your tush!
An arctic grouse kept warm inside a house
Might lay soft-boiled eggs.
A komodo dragon can pull you by wagon, man,
If it bit off your legs.

The giant sloth and luna moth
Are extinct and a myth,
A defanged snake is a cruel mistake
All it can do is "hith."
Wombats lack height, burrow all through the night,
Then spend all day in bed.
Sitting atop a giraffe would be good for a laugh,
If I didn't bonk my head.

THE REPEAT SYMBOL

At the end of some songs, instead of a double line like this:

You might see a double line with dots like this:

Those two dots indicate that you must go back to the song's beginning (or any other point indicated) and start playing from there.

Replace "poison arrow frog" with "long-ear, hog-nosed bat" and then...

...replace "plain old dog" with something like "world-class cat" or "t'riffic cat."

EQUAL REPRESENTATION FOR FELINES

RHYTHM AND STRUMMING

Rhythm, in music, refers to a steady beat of time. On the ukulele, rhythm is kept by the speed of your strumming. Here are some stroke suggestions to help you figure out some different rhythms.

Thumb Stroke
The Thumb Stroke consists of a single strum downwards with the fleshy tip of your thumb. You do so only once per measure or where ever a chord change is indicated. The effect is very gentle, and is good for soft and slow songs.

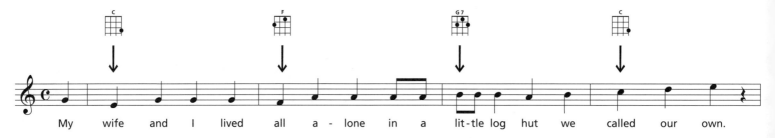

Simple Stroke
The Simple Stroke consists of two downwards strums per measure using only your index finger. This stroke has twice as many strums as the Thumb Stroke, so is better for a slightly faster song.

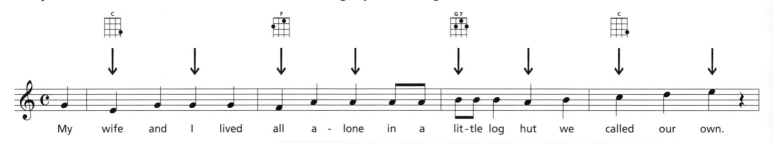

Common Stroke
The Common Stroke combines a down and an up strum. Like the name suggests, this is a common stroke, and probably the one you'll use most. In this example, try not to throw in an extra strum at the eighth notes (at "in a" and "little").

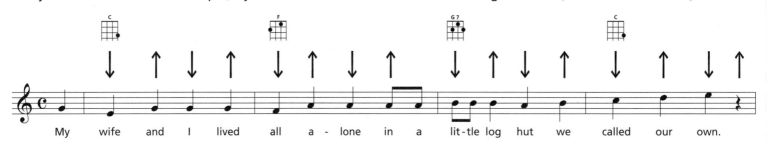

Bounce Stroke
The Bounce Stroke has a slightly more complicated pattern. Using your index finger, strum down, then down again, then up, and then down twice more. This stroke gives a nice bouncy feel to the rhythm and is good for lively songs.

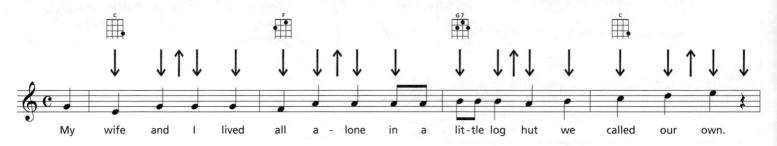

CHORD FAMILY: D MAJOR

Practice playing these chords as indicated on the music below. Strum once for each chord diagram or stroke mark (/). Concentrate more on smooth changes than on speed.

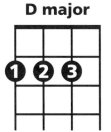
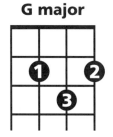
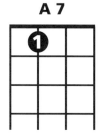

CHORD CHANGING EXERCISE

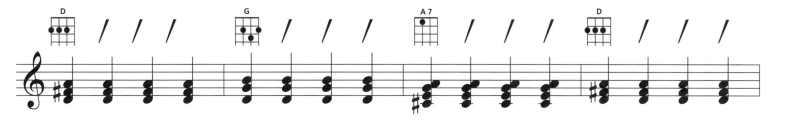
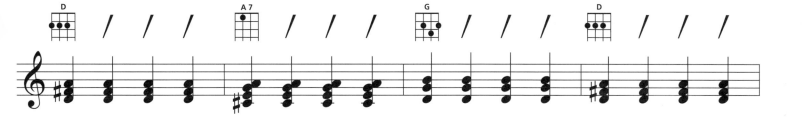
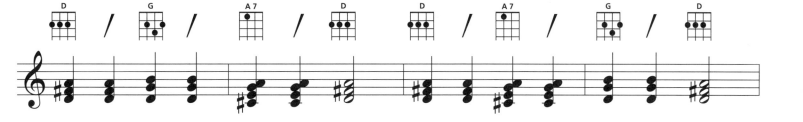
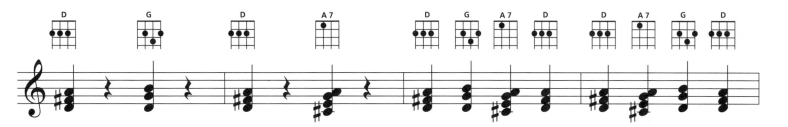

Here is a song that mixes melody playing with chord playing. The first 17 measures are plucked as a melody, the remaining measures are strummed as chords. You can do the same thing for any song. It gives a nice variation to the sound of your playing and it will teach you any unfamiliar melody.

My Love for You Is a Gaga Gugu

J. Connors

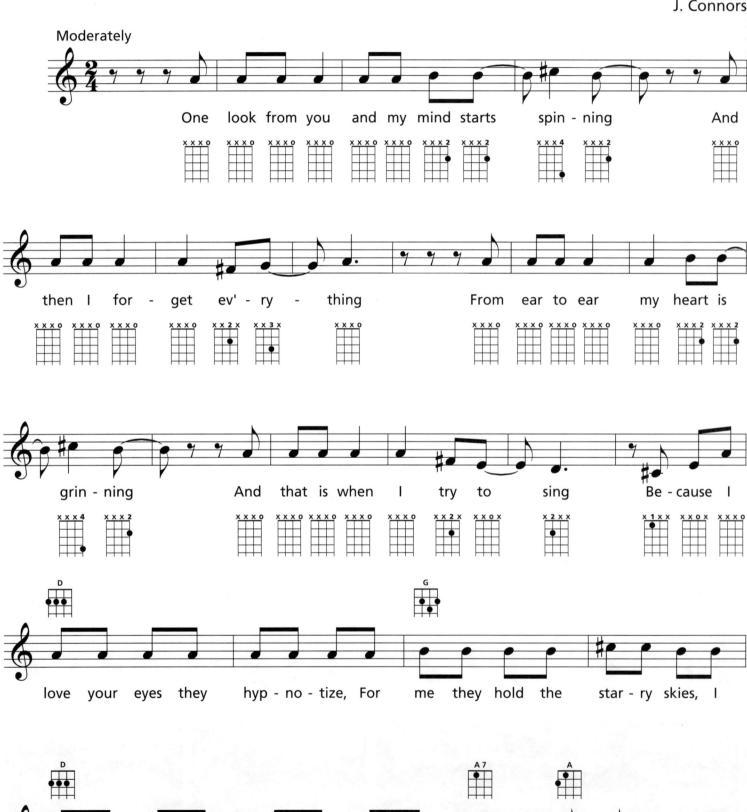

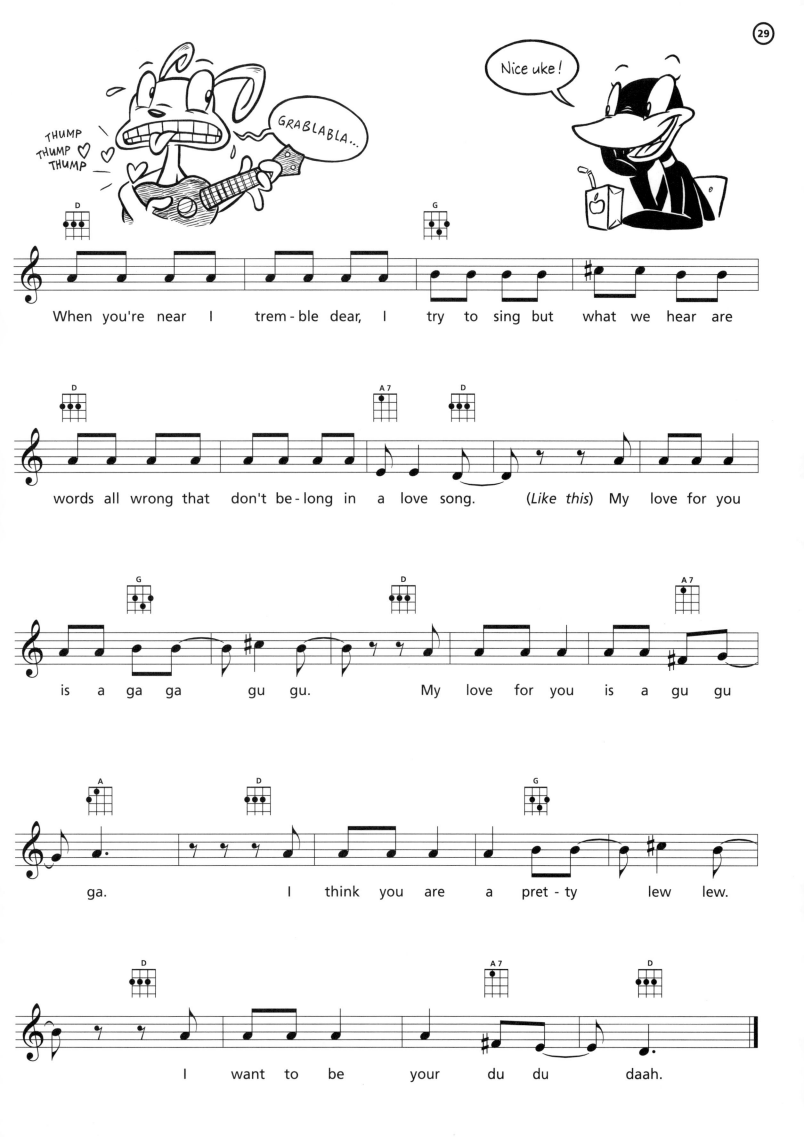

TRANSPOSING

Sometimes a song may feel too high or too low for you to sing easily. When that is the case, you can **transpose** the song into a different key. This means you replace one chord family for another. You will have to replace each chord with its proper counterpart. *Little Brown Jug* transposed from the key of C to the key of F would look like this:

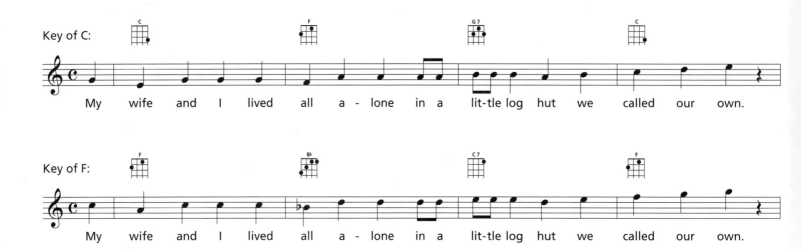

Remember: if you transpose one chord in a song, you must transpose them all. Use the chart below as a reference when transposing the songs in this book.

CHORD FAMILY	RELATED MAJOR CHORDS			RELATED MINOR CHORDS		
C	C	F	G7	Am	Dm	E7
D	D	G	A7	Bm	Em	F#7
E	E	A	B7	C#m	F#m	G#7
F	F	B♭	C7	Dm	Gm	A7
G	G	C	D7	Em	Am	B7
A	A	D	E7	F#m	Bm	C#7
B	B	E	F#7	G#m	C#m	D#7

Although our exercises only include the three major chords of each chord family, a chord family can include more chords. The chart above includes the related minor chords of each family.

CHORD FAMILY: G MAJOR

Practice playing these chords as indicated on the music below. Strum once for each chord diagram or stroke mark (/). Concentrate more on smooth changes than on speed.

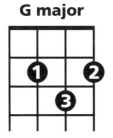
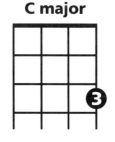
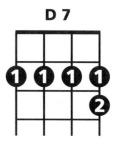

CHORD CHANGING EXERCISE

Although some people think ukuleles are good only for old-time and novelty tunes, many performers have used the ukulele in rock and roll. Here's a song you can try with a little rock in it.

The Mongoose Shuffle

J. Connors

CHORD FAMILY: A MAJOR

Practice playing these chords as indicated on the music below. Strum once for each chord diagram or stroke mark (/). Concentrate more on smooth changes than on speed.

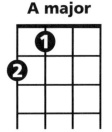
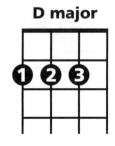
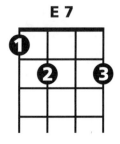

CHORD CHANGING EXERCISE

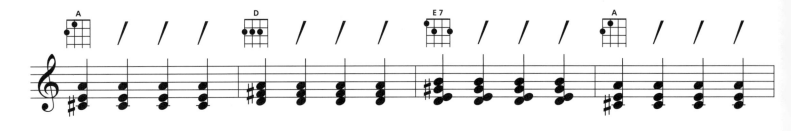

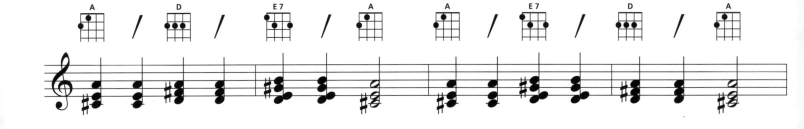
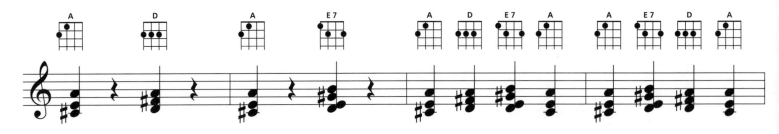

Your Momma Wears Army Boots

J. Connors

This song is set to the tune of the Delmore Brothers' *Deep River Blues* which they originally composed some years earlier as *Big River Blues*. *Deep River Blues* itself was often performed alongside the Brothers' *Brown's Ferry Blues* by Doc Watson in his own arrangement. Other versions of this song include *Wet Breetches Blues*, which borrowed heavily from *Itchy Squirrel Blues*, and 1939's *Who Ate My Pie Blues*.

Ok, those last three titles are made up. But it is true that traditional and folk tunes evolve over the years as they get passed from performer to performer and from generation to generation. Now it is your turn to get into the act.

Old Lunchroom Blues

traditional, arranged with new words by J. Connors

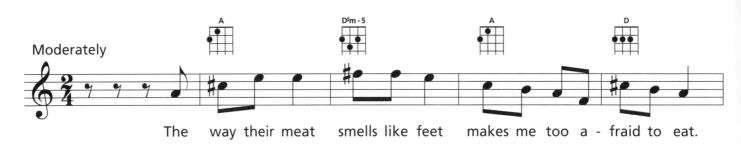
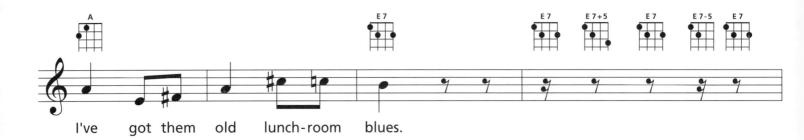
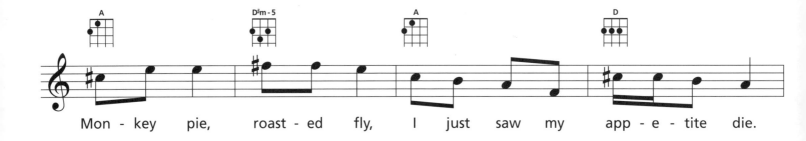
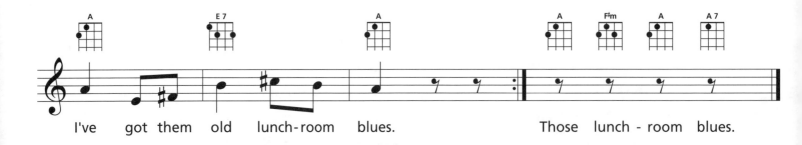

Make up your own lyrics and tack them on. Here are a few to get you started:

Gym sock stew	Dirt soufflé	I lost my nerve
And tide pool brew	With Poupon Grey	When I saw them serve
What a disgusting menu...	I'd sooner eat a pile of hay...	Worms and grubs as an hors d'oeurve...
I've got those old lunchroom blues.	I've got those old lunchroom blues.	I've got those old lunchroom blues.

UKULELE PUZZLES

The letters in the names on the Ukulele Hall of Fame marquee have been mixed up. Can you unscramble the letters to figure out who was really inducted?

Little Fly has gotten caught in this uke's soundhole, can you help her find a safe way out?

How many differences can you find in these two pictures?

Match the word that rhymes with "uke" to its definition:

cuke	a ghost or spy
Dubuque	a jukebox
duke	a town in Iowa
fluke	a crazy person
juke	a French comic book cowboy hero
kook	a narrow hat with a turned-up brim
Lucky Luke	to scold
rebuke	a cucumber
spook	a whale's tail fin or a bit of good luck
toque	the guy higher than a marquis

INTRODUCTIONS, ENDINGS & FLOURISHES

Introductions, endings, and flourishes are what add a little pepper to your playing. As you practice and learn new songs, these kinds of things will naturally suggest themselves to you. You should keep a notebook and jot down these ideas as they occur to you. They are worth practicing because besides adding a professional layer to your talent, they are fun to goof with and let evolve.

Introductions

An easy way to create an introduction for a song is by playing the melody line once before you begin strumming and singing. You can select a part from the verse or from the chorus, it doesn't have to be long but should be recognizable as a familiar part of the melody.

If playing the melody doesn't sound quite right, you can strum once through the song's chords without singing. Play the chords slowly at first, then pick up the tempo to match the song's speed just before going back to the start and singing.

Simple Effects

There are many different noises you can make with your uke, here are a few:

Bubble Pop	smack the sound hole (gently) with the open palm of your right hand
Bongo Drum	position your right hand as you would for picking, but let your fingers rest on your uke's body, use your thumb to drum a ryhthm just above the strings
Slide	pluck a string and then slide your finger along the fingerboard to make a note "slide" higher or lower.
Tremolo	pluck a string and then vary the pressure in your fretting finger to make the note you plucked waver

Endings and Flourishes

Here are some little musical devices that you can throw into your playing:

The Bluesy Bye-Bye

This is a good ending to a song in A major. You can play it two ways: as chords, or as a melody. If you want to play it as chords, follow this first example. For a good blues effect, slide your fingers from one position to the next.

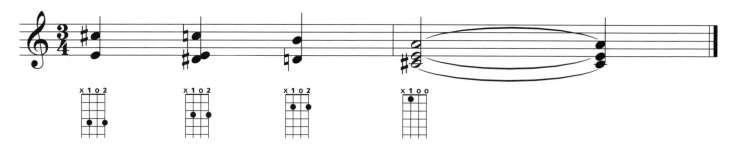

Playing these notes as a melody is simple. Fret the strings as you would for the chords above, but pluck the notes one at a time:

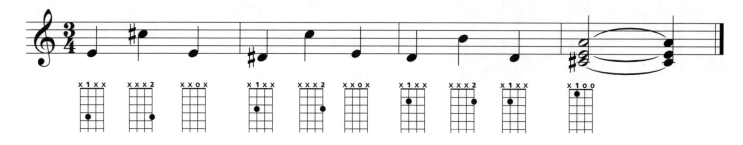

The Stoogey Sayonara

Here is a ditty used at the end of various songs.

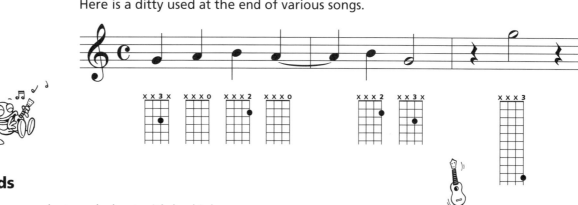

Good Evening Friends

This is a good ending to any song, but works best with bad jokes. Try it out for yourself. "Hey, I went downtown to buy some snoo." "What's snoo?" "Nothing, what's new with you?"...

The Swanee Shuffle

This is a fun little flourish to throw in the song *Old Folks at Home* *(page 21)* right after the lines "Far, far away" and "Sadly I roam".

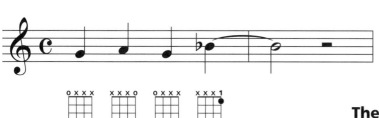

Shave and a Haircut

Two bits!

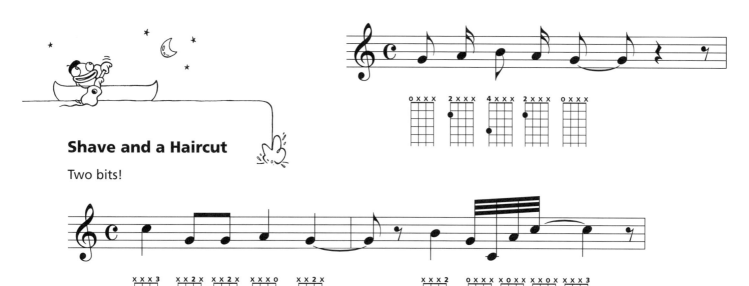

Look familiar? It's the C major chord. Only thing is, the notes are spread out and we hold the final C for an extra beat. Try experimenting with the tempo of these last four notes.

The Big Finish

You can tack this ending on to any song that ends with either a C major or G seventh chord.

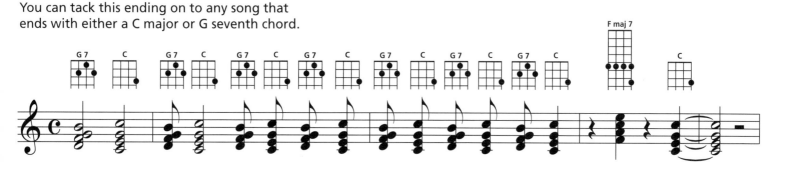

CHORD FAMILY: B MAJOR

Practice playing these chords as indicated on the music below. Strum once for each chord diagram or stroke mark (/). Concentrate more on smooth changes than on speed.

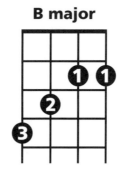
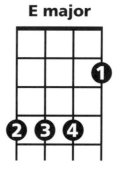
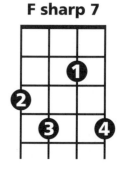

CHORD CHANGING EXERCISE

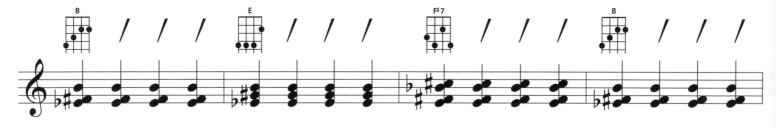
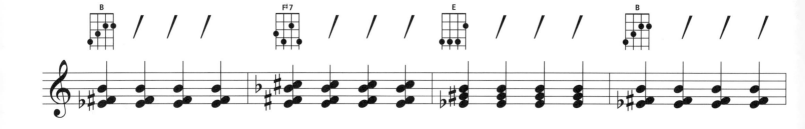

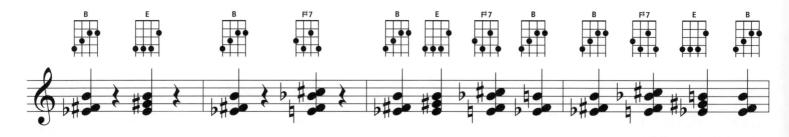

CHORD FAMILY: E MAJOR

Practice playing these chords as indicated on the music below. Strum once for each chord diagram or stroke mark (/). Concentrate more on smooth changes than on speed.

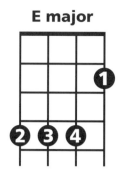
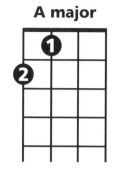
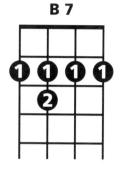

CHORD CHANGING EXERCISE

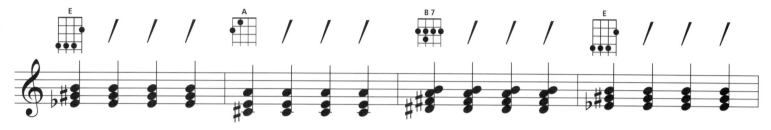
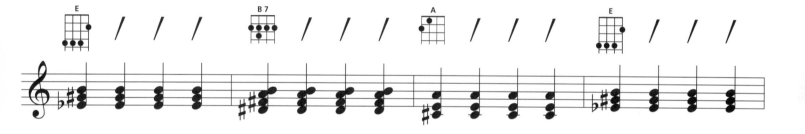
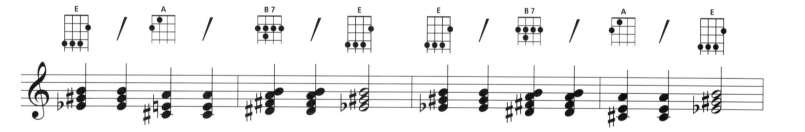
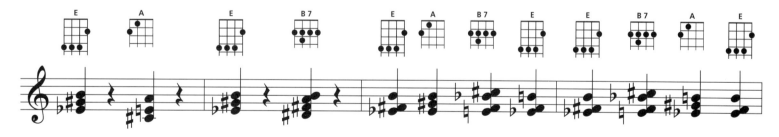

This is a song from 1876 written by Henry Clay Work. It was because of this song that those large clocks came to be called "Grandfather Clocks." The song is usually sung with a very deliberate "tick-tock-tick-tock" tempo, though speeding it up a little is fun also.

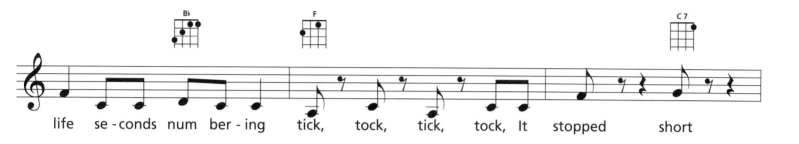
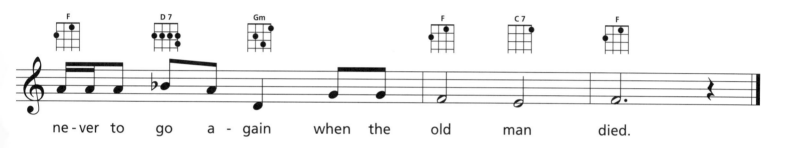

I'm watching its pendulum swing to and fro.
Many hours had he spent while a boy.
And in childhood and manhood the clock seemed to know,
And to share both his grief and his joy.
For it struck twenty four
When he entered at the door
With a blooming and beautiful bride.
But it stopped short, never to go again
When the old man died...

My grandfather said that of those he could hire,
Not a servant so faithful he found;
For it wasted no time, and had but one desire –
At the close of each week to be wound.
And it kept in its place
Not a frown upon its face,
And its hands never hung by its side.
But it stopped short, never to go again
When the old man died...

BE A UKULELE HERO

So now you are an accomplished ukulele player, you are the envy of your peers and the delight of your parents. So now what?

Take your talents down to your local retirement center and put on a show for the seniors. Many of the popular songs of your grandparents' and great-grandparents' age are quite easy to learn and master on the ukulele.

You'd be hard pressed to find a more appreciative audience. But just in case, don't go there at dinner time or any other time when they may have tomatoes at hand.

TIPS ON SHOWMANSHIP

Playing any instrument in front of an audience can take some nerve. Fortunately, with a ukulele you have an immediate advantage – everybody likes the uke. But don't rely entirely on the uke's charms, here are a few tips to remember while performing:

Sing Loudly
Having trouble keeping your voice in the right key and in tune? You'll find it's easier to sing along if you raise your voice slightly. Don't be shy and whisper. Belt out that tune. If your singing stinks, play loudly to cover it up.

Play Slowly and Clearly
Most of the mistakes a person makes can be attributed to playing too quickly. People tend to speak and play faster when they are nervous. Try playing slower until you are confident you have it. *Then* speed it up.

Play Through Your Mistakes
Don't stop and apologize every time you strum the wrong chord. Instead, just keep playing. The audience probably won't notice your mistake unless you draw attention to it, so smile and keep strumming!

Keep Your Uke in Tune
The ukulele can fall out of tune pretty easily, especially if you're hammering out an energetic tune. Between songs tune your uke by ear, and while tuning tell your audience a joke or two. And of course...

Practice
As with anything, the more you do it, the better you will get. Practice playing in front of your family and friends as often as they are willing to listen. Have a friend who plays uke or another instrument? Practice together and make up your own duets.

IMPROVISING MELODIES

When you get better at playing chords while singing, you may find yourself humming or singing a slightly different melody than what you meant to play. What you are doing is improvising, which basically means "making it up as you go along." Improvising can be a lot of fun as there are no rules. You can follow these suggestions to fine tune your improvising skills:

- Get yourself a tape recorder and find a nice quiet area to play.

- Record yourself strumming a song several times in a row (so you don't have to rewind as often). Then play back the recording.

- As you listen to the strumming pick out notes to play a melody.

- Choose the melody that you like best and build on that one.

It's inevitable, once you are seen playing the ukulele, someone will start yelling, "Hey! Play *Tip-Toe Through the Tulips! TIP-TOE!!*" Why is this such a popular song for the uke? The song was written by Joe Burke and Al Dubin in the twenties and used in Warner Brothers' *Gold Diggers of Broadway* (1929). Although it was a popular song and a sheet music top seller, it was made a ukulele standard by Herbert Khaury, better known as Tiny Tim, when he released it on his 1968 album, *God Bless Tiny Tim*. His recording became a top-twenty hit, and *Tip-Toe* became tied forever to the fascinatingly strange man and his ukulele.

When someone starts yelling at you to play *Tip-Toe Through the Tulips* you can tell him or her you don't know that song, but you know something a bit like it. Sing this song to them, but replace the name "Jackson" with theirs.

Jackson Is a Monkey
(sung to the tune of *Tip-Toe Through the Tulips*)

And that, my friend, is the end of your training.
Thanks for buying my book, have fun with your uke.

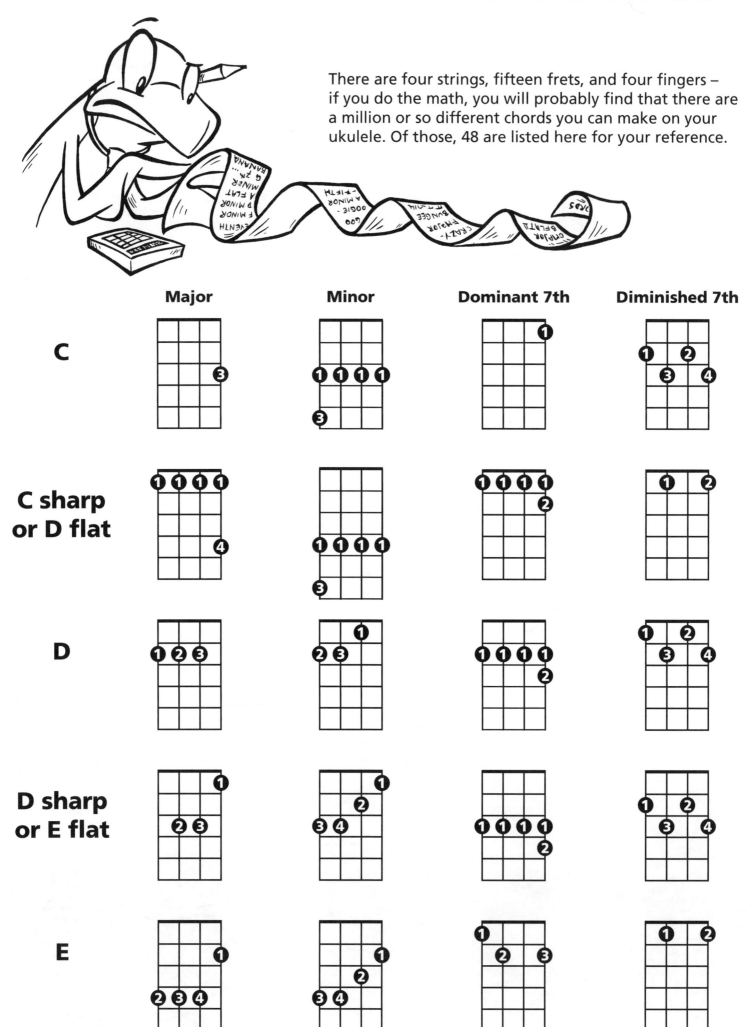

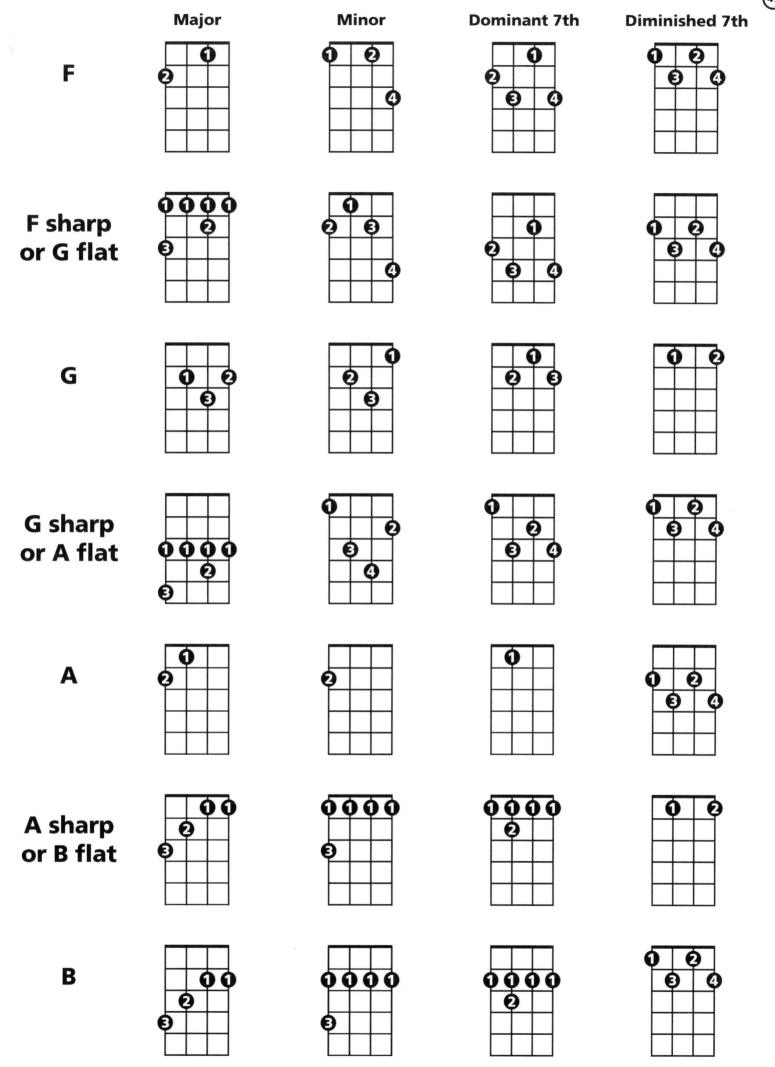

UKULELE PUZZLE ANSWERS

page 23 - Mystery Tune:

Excerpt from Beethoven's *Ninth Symphony* "Ode to Joy"

page 33 - Dance Hall Puzzler:

Left to right from top left: The Mexican Hat Dance, The Lindy Hop or Bunny Hop, The Boney Maroney or Dinosaur, The Twist, Break Dancing, The Bump or Can Can, The Mashed Potato

page 37 - Hall of Fame Scrambler:

Froog Be Germy = George Formby
Rocky Mes = Roy Smeck
Beak Wing Ninny Ha = King Benny Nawahi
Steak In Rue = Ernest Kaui
Askamka A Mule = Samuel Kamaka
Clad W Differs = Cliff Edwards
Great Hurry Fod = Arthur Godfrey
Try Her Hauberk = Herbert Khaury
Brings Me In Yeah = May Singhi Breen

page 37 - Definitions Match:

cuke = a cucumber
Dubuque = a town in Iowa
duke = the guy higher than a marquis
fluke = a whale's tail fin or a bit of good luck
juke = a jukebox
kook = a crazy person
Lucky Luke = a French comic book cowboy hero
rebuke = to scold
spook = a ghost or spy
toque = a narrow hat with a turned-up brim

For those of you who were wondering, a **kakapo** is an endangered species of ground parrot native to New Zealand (they don't play ukulele). Take care of the planet! Reduce, reuse, recycle and protect that kakapo!

The book ends here, but your playing doesn't have to.
Go to Ukulele Boogaloo for songs, lessons, and other fun stuff.

www.alligatorboogaloo.com/uke